Animal Body Coverings

Why do
owls and other
birds have
feathers?

Holly Beaumont

raintree

a Capstone company — publishers for children

Raintree is an imprint of Capstone Global Library Limited, a company incorporated in England and Wales having its registered office at 7 Pilgrim Street, London EC4V 6LB – Registered company number: 6695582

www.raintree.co.uk
myorders@raintree.co.uk

Edited by Clare Lewis and Kristen Mohn
Designed by Richard Parker
Picture research by Svetlana Zhurkin
Production by Victoria Fitzgerald
Originated by Capstone Global Library
Printed and bound in China by Leo Paper Products Ltd

ISBN 978 1 406 29922 9
19 18 17 16 15
10 9 8 7 6 5 4 3 2 1

British Library Cataloguing in Publication Data
A full catalogue record for this book is available from the British Library.

Acknowledgements
We would like to thank the following for permission to reproduce photographs: Dreamstime: Dave M. Hunt Photography, 21, 23, Jhernan124, 13; iStockphoto: summersetretrievers, 9; Newscom: Photoshot/NHPA/Joe Blossom, 17; Shutterstock: Aliaksei Hintau, back cover (right), 16, 22 (top right), Chantal de Bruijne, 7, Critterbiz, 15, Dave Montreuil, 14, Dennis W. Donohue, 11, Erni, 8, fullempty, 4 (bottom), HHsu, 23 (rabbits), Lee319, cover (top), LesPalenik, 19, Marcin Sylwia Ciesielski, 18, 22 (bottom), 23, Mark Bridger, 5, meaofoto, 20, mlorenz, cover (bottom), monticello, 4 (top right), Oleksandr Chub, 23 (velvet), PeterVrabel, 23 (peacocks), Sorapop Udomsri, 6, 23, Steve Allen, 4 (top left), TheX, 10, 22 (top left), Tomatito, back cover (left), 12, Tracy Starr (feathers), cover and throughout

We would like to thank Michael Bright for his invaluable help in the preparation of this book.

Every effort has been made to contact copyright holders of material reproduced in this book. Any omissions will be rectified in subsequent printings if notice is given to the publisher.

All the internet addresses (URLs) given in this book were valid at the time of going to press. However, due to the dynamic nature of the internet, some addresses may have changed, or sites may have changed or ceased to exist since publication. While the author and publisher regret any inconvenience this may cause readers, no responsibility for any such changes can be accepted by either the author or the publisher.

Contents

Some words are shown in bold, **like this**. You can find them in the picture glossary on page 23.

Which animals have feathers?

Birds have feathers. Birds have beaks and wings. They also lay eggs.

Different birds have different types of feathers.

Owls are birds. They have large, flat faces and big eyes.

What are feathers?

Feathers are made from the same **material** as your skin, hair and fingernails.

Feathers grow out of the skin of birds.

Feathers can be soft and fluffy.
They can be strong and straight.

Different feathers do different jobs.

Do feathers keep birds warm?

Feathers protect birds from chilly nights and cold winters.

Birds fluff up their feathers to trap air against their skin. This air warms up and keeps the birds warm.

This great-horned owl has lots of thick feathers.

They help it to stay warm at night.

How do feathers help birds fly?

Most birds use their feathers to help them fly.

Strong wing feathers help birds take off and fly through the air. Long tail feathers help them to steer.

wing feathers

tail feathers

Owl feathers are soft and **velvety**.

They help owls to fly quietly as they hunt for food.

Do feathers keep birds dry?

Some water birds, such as ducks and gulls, have very waterproof feathers.

They stop the birds from getting too wet and cold.

Owls do not like flying in the rain.
Their feathers are not very waterproof.

They get soggy and heavy.
This makes flying hard work.

Do feathers help birds hide?

Some birds use their feathers to hide from **predators**.

This nightjar nests on the ground. Its brown feathers make it hard to see.

This snowy owl is getting ready to pounce on its **prey**.

Its white feathers make it hard to spot against the snow

What else are feathers for?

Some birds don't want to hide.

For male birds, bright feathers are a good way of getting noticed.

This peacock is hoping to attract a **mate** with his colourful display.

Female birds are often less colourful.

This peahen needs to stay hidden while she cares for her eggs.

How do feathers change as birds get older?

Many baby birds can't fly straight away.

They spend their first weeks in the nest. Their soft **downy** feathers help to keep them warm.

The young birds' wing muscles get stronger. The birds grow long flight feathers.

Soon they are ready to leave the nest and fly for the first time.

How do birds take care of their feathers?

Pests such as lice can eat and damage bird feathers. This can make the bird ill.

Feathers are very important to birds. They have to look after them.

This owl is **preening**.

It is using its beak to clean its feathers. It checks the feathers for any damage.

Feathers quiz

Which of these feathers are for keeping birds warm?

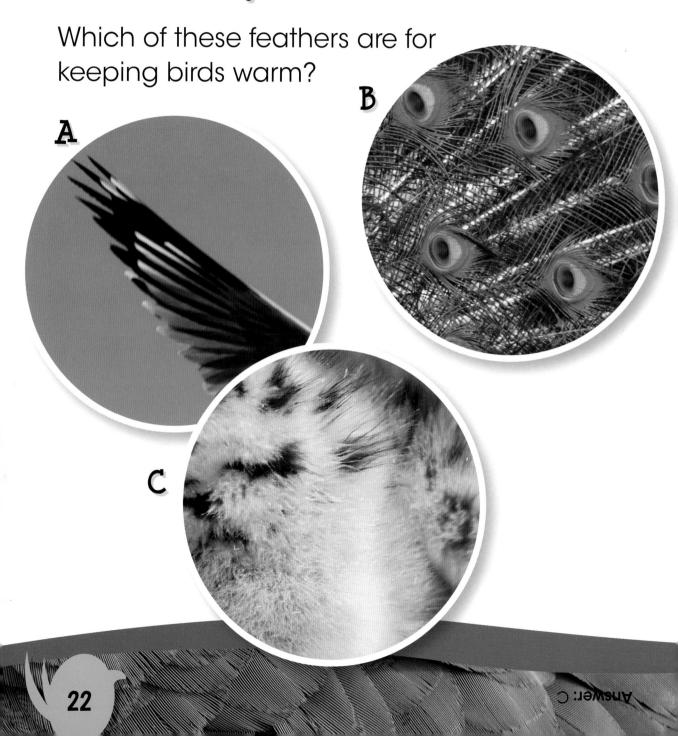

A

B

C

Answer: C

Picture glossary

 **down**   soft, fluffy feathers covering baby birds

 **mate**   male and female partners that come together to make babies

 **material**   substance from which something is made

 **predator**   animal that hunts and eats other animals

 **preen**   to tidy and clean feathers with a beak

 **prey**   animal that is hunted and eaten by another animal

 **velvety**   feeling like velvet fabric, soft to the touch

Find out more

Websites

www.bbc.co.uk/nature/life/Owl
Discover owl facts, watch videos and hear the latest news.

www.barnowl.co.uk/page33.asp
Visit this barn owl centre and view videos showing barn owls in the nest.

kids.sandiegozoo.org/animals/birds/peacock
See more of the peacock, the show-off of the bird world.

Books

Barn Owls, Patricia Whitehouse (Raintree, 2010)

Owls (Animals are Amazing), Valerie Bodden (Franklin Watts, 2013)

Owls (Usborne Beginners), Emily Bone (Usborne, 2013)

Index